War Food

War Food

Milica Mijatović

SOUTHWORDeditions

First published in 2023
by Southword Editions
The Munster Literature Centre
Frank O'Connor House, 84 Douglas Street
Cork, Ireland

Set in Adobe Caslon 12pt

ISBN 978-1-915573-01-8

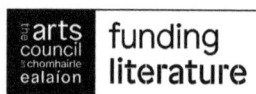

arts
council
chomhairle
ealaíon

funding
literature

Contents

Ex-Yugoslav War, 1991-1995

Sometimes I wish I was there during the war.
I'd be me but I wouldn't be my parents' daughter—
I'd be their friend, part of their in-crowd, laughing
when they laugh, ducking for cover when they duck.

Sometimes I wish it so badly I forget I'm in America, find
myself seeing body parts on the ground, watch as Kosta
gathers them in his hands. I realize he's tending to fallen
apples, and I stifle my scream. Later when he offers

me the fruit, I don't eat it. In my dreams I'm more vividly
dodging death by war. It's not that I want to die. It's guilt
for not being there, guilt for writing of it, guilt for fleeing.
I keep scouring history books, poems, cemeteries,

photos, voices, villages, wrinkles, graffitied walls, bridges.
I keep looking for whom I'm to be ducking from.
In my imagination I carry no weapons, I see no enemies.
Who is bombing us? Who are we fighting?

How many of us have died wondering? I wish I could've
been there to lift a wounded soldier's head, asked
Šta radimo mi ovdje? and listened. Maybe he'd know.
The problem with three-sided wars is the assumption

that two sides must be wrong. The problem with war
is the need for one side to win. Sometimes I wish
I was there when they tallied the dead and did or did not
fumble to declare a victor. Who is it that won?

The silence that follows creates a vacuum for anyone
to howl into. I guess the loudest wins. In any case, this war
follows me like a street dog, hungry and alone, leaves me
wondering where the bones and land mines are buried.

Donji Žabar

Back when everyone was still alive,
we'd gather in the village, sit under
the vinograd, and drink my aunt's
homemade rose juice until the jugs
were completely empty, our tongues
so thorny. All my cousins would
rush to play with the sun as long
as they could, but on those rosy days,
I couldn't move. I'd lie there, head
in the shade, and listen to my uncle's
raspy voice tell the same war stories
he'd been telling even before the war.
I listened less to hear and more to
remember Ujak Milje's smoky laugh,
Baka Zorka's shaky voice, the dog's
bark. I'd listen and daydream about
roses blooming in my stomach. Now,
just when I think I can't hear them,
I cough up handfuls of red petals.

Residue

In a dream, Deda Savo tells me he misses me,
but we've never met, not in this life, not even almost.

In the morning, I run to his tombstone candles in hand,
climb uneven ground, weave through the dead people,

find him sitting there with family, weeds all around.
Plopping beside him, I tell him I've missed him too,

catch him up on my life although he knows everything
already. Deda looks at me as he always looks at me,

except he has never looked at me, but we look nonetheless.
I tell him about grandma, how she's still living, how she's still

alone. He knows that too because he's still dead, still alone.
I tell him people keep dying, and there's almost no one left

in the *selo*. The earth keeps eating his house, a little piece
there, one here, and I'm scared of the day it's just gone.

I light the candles, and we sit in silence as they burn.
After a few minutes, I thank him for listening, tell him

I'm so happy he didn't forget me, promise I'll be back as soon
as I can. I half skip down the hill, across the field, through

the village to my car. Pavle waves to me from his *vinograd*
as I drive away, windows down, fingers sticky from the wax.

Oj Golube, Moj Golube

I was born to pigeons cooing.
Was the war over then? Not sure,
officially maybe yes, but Mama

gave birth in a windowless hospital.
And by windowless, I mean the windows
had been shattered by bullets or shrapnel,

so the draft almost killed all of us.
The pregnancy ward was one room,
beds like soldiers on the front line,

babies like bullets aimed at the next
one hundred years. I asked Mama
if she thought she was going to die.

She said the pigeons were everywhere,
and everything smelled bad. I asked
if anyone died. She said not everyone

noticed this big pigeon in the corner,
gray and blue, *mora da je majka,* poised
and happy. Warm. Sometimes I think

I hear cooing, a sort of calling home.
It's as if the pigeons remember
Mama holding me til a nurse took me

because Mama was coughing, sick.
Both of us lived. It had to have been
the pigeons. They were our peace treaties,

our ceasefires. One time a man told me
every pigeon you see is a prayer—*svaki
golub je molitva*—and it made me wonder

if Mama ever saw any pigeons at all.

Grenade, Dream

I dreamt Tata jumped on a grenade,
and the grenade was me. I didn't go off,
but I could've. I could've killed my father.

The Gift

Picture this: a little gift wrapped in aluminum foil
sitting on top of a war tank's gun, the gun carefully
directed at a second story balcony, the balcony bare
except for some clothes hanging on the clothesline,
the clothes on the line drooping enough to graze the gift
on the gun & worry the tank driver, the tank driver
maneuvering the obstacles & waiting for his lover
to come out, the lover inside spinning & unspinning
herself into photographs of her soldier, the photographs
curling at the edges & wincing in potential memoriam,
in potential memoriam chuckling at the assumption
that in memoriam itself is potential, the potential to love
pulling the tank driver from his turret & his lover
from her longing, the longing leaving for a second
as she reaches for him & not the gift, the gift long
forgotten decades later, the gift its own in memoriam.

Pored Rijeke Brke

Kada prodješ kraj pijace
i kada osjetiš onaj miris
svježih banana pomješan sa
mirisom domaćeg paradajza
i tek ubranih narandži,
pomisli na mene i kako smo
zajedno prolazili tim putem
da umanjimo, makar malo,
zadah koji dolazi iz rijeke;
da zaboravimo, samo nakratko,
na ratište koje nas čeka preko
mosta; da udahnemo, bar na tren,
vazduh ove zemlje i osjetimo
kako nam sok iz narandže
kvasi ruke dok je gulimo.

By the Brka River

When you walk by the market,
and when you notice that smell
of fresh bananas mixed
with home-grown tomatoes
and newly picked oranges,
think of me, and how we
used to walk that way together
to, at least a little, cover the rank
smell coming from the river;
to forget, just for a while,
about the battlefield waiting
for us across the bridge;
to, just for a moment,
inhale the air of this earth
and feel how the juice
from the orange wets our hands
as we press our fingers
into the skin.

City Tree

Grandpa's house is an orange, growing
from the street branch and sucking up the light.
The city tree took three years to start bearing
some fruit, but it doesn't look all that right.
Some of the branches are dead, closed
til construction can come again, exposed
to zinc deficiencies and other blights.
The neighboring fruit dried up quickly—
homes once vibrant in color are now empty;
soil, needing water, absorbs it from soggy cigarettes.

Strawberries

We ate them in the field by the stream
after old man Jocika passed. Funerals,
something we were good at. Someone
made a joke about Jocika's mangled hands,
the way he would pretend to eat his fingers,
master of the noses & thumbs game.
He used to make us laugh. He used to tell us
stories about how he lost his fingers, each
finger a different story, and each story
different every time. The ring on his ring finger
choked his finger to death; he woke one morning
to a missing thumb, searched for days, found
it in his backyard, riddled with ants; he won
first place in a pinky finger beauty contest,
was asked to sit still for a mold, couldn't wait
long, so he cut his pinky off, donated it,
and now it sits in all its glory in a museum
in Helsinki. His contribution to western society.
We grew up when we realized what actually
happened to his hands, and some time after,
his heart burst, the same way strawberries do
when you bite into them just right.

I'm looking for you

even today   under blankets   in hands
        on branches   Sometimes I go to the store
and chase you   between shelves   hoping you'll
        recognize me   hoping you'll   come   home
but actually what's left isn't a home isn't even
        a wall   and I want to tell   you   to stay
right where you are   because here   in this city
        on this street   honey often   goes bad
Maybe there's something   still   in the air
        buzzing   waiting   Maybe it's really
something   in us   the living   the almost dead
        that leaves us   gasping   for anything
but the future   leaves me looking   for your ghost
        among wreckage   in jars   full of honey

HUMAN HEAD, DREAM

A land mine found him,
and he came back to his fiancé
as a bodiless soldier, only
his head left functioning.
The two of them married
in my backyard, grenade pins
for rings, except he had no
fingers because he had no hands
or arms or shoulders or legs.
And when it came to the kiss,
I picked up his swollen head
and held it to his new wife's lips.

VUK

Mi rađamo vukove, nadajući
se da će barem jedan preživjeti.
Ali šanse su male—niko ne želi
divlju životinju kao gosta za večeru
ili kao prijatelja ili kao ljubavnika.
Nema šume u kojoj nismo bili,
ni mjeseca kojeg nismo pljunuli.
Proganjajte nas cijelu noć ako hoćete—
kad svane, biće da smo mi lovljeni, a vi ubijeni.

Vuk

We give birth to wolves,
hoping one of them will live.
But chances are slim—nobody
wants wild animal as dinner guest
or friend or lover. There's no wood
we haven't been, no moon we haven't
spit on. Stalk us all night if you will—
by morning, it'll be us hunted, you killed.

To the American woman who praises NATO for bombing Serbia, land of brutes!

I am a brute   yes a brute   I can eat
          you whenever   I want
won't think   twice   about it   You
          are shocked   but you made
me this way   This is who   you need me
          to be   Go home and tell
everyone there   I am   120 pounds
          of savagery   and when they
ask where   you found   me   say
          I was buried   under rubble
charred black   faceless   7 months pregnant
          or say   you found   me
on the toilet   hit by shrapnel   bled
          on my parents   a child only
3 years old   or say   you collected
          my dismembered   body
picked up   my arms   legs   hands
          and head   couldn't put
it back together   like it used   to be
          and when they   ask if they
won   you shake   their hands   proudly
          for they   and you   have
subdued the brute   but they   and you
          have made me   hungry

War Food

Except for this, there are no more war
stories left to tell. I've tasted thunder
like you wouldn't believe. Forests
have grown in my palms, and men
have carved men into trees. See all
these stains on my skin? I'm rotting.
An apple you shouldn't pick. I've
scavenged for friends' body parts
in fields we used to race in, trying
to outrun eagles above us. How
could we have known? Scattered
puzzle pieces and broken trinkets.
The last lesson as grasshoppers feed.

Aftermath

Love, did you know not one day is birthless?
　　Proves days don't exist as objects we can pocket
& savor later. The sun has been stuck in your throat.
No one has knocked on our sky in months—
　　do we not matter anymore?

Last night I threw a rock at a dog & nothing. Maybe
we're both ghosts. Wonder how many friends he lost,
　　how many of my friends he carried in his mouth.
I walked over to him, and he bolted. What have we done?

I used to sleep on a radiator. Hate having time to dream.
　　War sleep is the best sleep until you almost
kill your father. What I'm trying to say is I'm alive.
And if I wish for anything, it's for you to be alive, too.
　　If I ever pocket a day, I'll save it for you.

Phantom Scar Syndrome

I can't find my scars, the ones that happened
before my birth, the one on Mama's left eyebrow,
on Tata's stomach, above his left ear, down his right leg.
Sometimes I wince, touch those places on my skin
where nothing is. I don't even know their stories, how
long they bled, who helped them home, how they felt.
My brain is relentless in the way its figments whisper
and make me believe I was there. Is this possible,
these phantom scars? Are there bullet fragments in me?

*

We've landed in America, after everything. I have scars
of my own, like the one time I said I fell onto a broken
Heineken bottle in the middle of some club and cut up
my right arm. I hid the cuts from my parents for weeks,
even bought some scar-erasing cream online. Tata found
out, investigated my arm and answers, told me they looked
like scars he'd seen before. I told him that's impossible.
Months later I'd catch him rubbing his right arm, wincing,
as if something were there but missing, unknown, lost.

WAR, DREAM

If you're quiet enough, you
can almost hear nothing,
the kind of nothing that scares
you into thinking you've gone
deaf, except you haven't
because your sister is screaming,
except she isn't even born yet,
and neither are you, but you're
definitely here, your tears
are bodies falling
only two klicks away,
you're here, and you're running
toward what looks like a finish
line, except here finishes
don't exist, and even though
you know whom you're running
from, you turn around to look
one last time at your burning
home, except it isn't your home,
it isn't even your war,
but you are here, and you grip
your chest because something
in there aches, but your sister
is screaming somewhere
in the distance, so you have no
time to grieve, not while the alarms
are sounding, not while the troops
are marching, not while your people
are watching, except no one
is here but you

Roots

Plums save people
from their loneliness,
so we plant plum trees
across the whole country
and pray for a time plums
don't have to worry about us.

I watch a young war veteran
drink from his paper bag
two benches to my left.
Bodies and bombs hide
in the green Sava
while plums shake.

He remembers everything
when he closes his eyes
because plums don't save.
But they never leave him—
"There, there," they whisper.
"You won't explode alone."

To The Man I Always Light A Candle For:

The moon rising looks like the back
of my late grandfather's head, or at least
that's what I think it'd be—splotchy and creased—
if he were conducting his Communist ways
among us still. I'd join his ranks any day,
marching by his side, sporting the black

and red checkered dress he once gave Mama,
who kept it throughout the years as a memory
of his voice. She often speaks of how trees
used to sing her to sleep, but the world is too
loud now. She was five when he turned blue,
and it was too late for the priest's psalm.

The morning of his funeral, people lined
the cemetery gates to honor a splendid man
whose young daughter down the hill ran,
smiling, little lilies in her hair. It was sunny
that day as people mixed their tea with honey
and talked of politics and family left behind.

The moon, turning its head in the navy sky,
is my grandfather, among us still. I see him
at night when the world barely hushes for the trees' hymn,
and I picture Mama running into his soft arms,
a little girl with lilies in her hair. Far from harm,
she walks with him as I walk with him now, eye to eye.

Novo Brčko

Baka's one-bedroom apartment is a bluedusk-colored
poem. Its pigeons coo me awake; city buses cradle me in
their wheels. The balconies—one in the bedroom, the other
in the living room—let just enough of the outside world
in. Soft shadows on the wall play hide-and-seek with
my dreams. I sleep on the pullout couch, brush my teeth
in the purple-tiled bathroom, eat on the wooden chairs Deda
bought a few centuries back. It's just my grandma and me.
We look through black-and-white photographs of her life—
I watch as she lingers over some, passes quickly over others.
She brings out Mama's wedding dress, and I put it on, twirl.
She cries. I sink into my book on the couch as the TV
hums just one octave above the refrigerator. It's bluedusk—
the sun is setting. The curtains walk with the wind, and
I remember Deda's impressive collection of pins. We run
out of drinking water, so I head down to the public fountain,
two empty jugs in my hand. I read the graffitied signs again,
mostly love declarations and nationalistic leanings. I climb
the two flights back home, Baka serves peaches and plums,
and we talk about the weather. There's enough hot water
to shower, and I listen to the 11p.m. bus from Beograd
zoom into the station. Baka plays a movie; tonight, it's *Ocean's
Eleven*. We doze through the action, murmur goodnight.
I head to my room, embrace the cool sheets as the old, drunk
men in the bar across the street sing some obscure battle song,
strum their guitars off-key, and I let them lull me to sleep.

ECHOES IN THE SAVA

Friendship is killing each other and reuniting
in the afterlife. Hate here is a different kind of hate.
We pretend to know anything about it, graffiti
our alliances on unimportant buildings
and abandoned war tanks. Do you know how many
mines are in the Sava? Sometimes we go swimming
for them. They were put there for somebody.
Best we find them, die as martyrs of a war
that'll never end, as friends harvested in the same
field under the same dry sun. Friendship is truest
here—in the look we give each other before plunging
into the water, headfirst, hunting for the thing
that divided our fathers. Friendship is emerging,
lungs in tow, finding each other alive one more time,
laughing, embracing. Then, diving in again.

PEDESTRIAN BRIDGE OVER THE TRAIN TRACKS IN BRČKO, BIH

I don't know when the bridge was built,
or when the trains stopped running, or which
side of the tracks was ours & which theirs,
or why they painted the bridge turquoise,
or why war is obsessed with lines, or who
graffitied one of the bridge railings
with "Teška vremena, prijatelju," or why
some cement steps are missing, or how.
But I know the tracks are a line, the war
a blur, the bridge a truth. I know the way
home is quickest across the tracks. I know
as kids we never went that way alone.
But one day the bridge became our meeting
place, our common ground, and we'd sit, you
with your name & me with mine. I'd say
This place makes me forget to be someone, and
you'd look at me bewildered—*All this place does
is make me be someone.* We were both stuck
adhering to lines drawn on our knuckles,
clenching our fists at the imaginary rumbling
of some train coming to prove us wrong.

"I TOKOM RATA, POGOTOVO TOKOM RATA, SMIJALI SMO SE"

Naslijedili smo smijeh od roditelja koji su morali da kopaju
na umornim koljenima da ga nadju; koji su morali čekati da dodje
struja ne bi li pročitali o njemu na svojim kožama, pa ga zapamtili
prije nego što se svijetla opet ugase. Smijeh, oni nam kažu,
je proljeće, je boja plave ptice, je poslednji gutljaj rakije, je tišina
izmedju zvuka bombe i eksplozije, je rupa u zidu kroz koju
ti drug plazi jezik, je selo tačno prije nego što starica popije čaj.
Uzmite smijeh, kažu nam, i pjevajte mu da zaspi jer lako
pobjegne, ali se ne boji mraka. Zato ga koristite kao pokrivač
čak i tokom toplih noći, prekrijte uši s njim kad se oglasi alarm,
i sačekajte da odjekne kroz zidove i generacije. Kad ga čujete,
sakrijte ga iza uha dok ne dodje vaš red da ga proslijedite.

"AND DURING THE WAR, ESPECIALLY DURING THE WAR, WE LAUGHED"

We inherited laughter from our parents who had to dig
for it on their tired knees; had to wait for the electricity
to switch on, so they could read about it on their skins,
memorize it before the lights flickered off again. Laughter,
they tell us, is spring, is the color blue jay, is the last sip
of a rakija shot, is the silence between the bomb sound
and the bomb explosion, is the hole in the wall your friend
sticks his tongue through as a joke, is the village right before
the old woman sips her tea. Take laughter, they say, and sing
it to sleep because it runs away easily, but it's not afraid
of the dark, so use it as a blanket even on warm nights,
cover your ears with it when the alarms sound, and wait
for it to echo through walls and generations. When you trip
over it, hide it behind your ear until it's your turn to pass it down.

Acknowledgements

Grateful acknowledgment is made to the following publications in which these poems first appeared, or will appear, sometimes in different versions:

Broadsided Press: "Donji Žabar"
Collateral: "War, Dream" and "I'm looking for you"
Consequence: "Aftermath" and "And during the war, especially during the war, we laughed"
Palette Poetry: "By the Brka River" and "Pored Rijeke Brke"
Plume: "Oj Golube, Moj Golube"
Santa Ana River Review: "Residue"
The Louisville Review: "Strawberries" and "Human Head, Dream"
The Night Heron Barks: "War Food" and "Roots"
Red Wheelbarrow: "Novo Brčko"
Rattle: "Pedestrian Bridge Under the Train Tracks in Brčko, BiH"

Much, much gratitude to Patrick Cotter, James O'Leary, and everyone at the Munster Literature Centre for believing in this book and in me.

I want to thank all of my professors and mentors for their support and guidance: Kevin Griffith, Lisette Gibson, Gail Mazur, Robert Pinsky, Karl Kirchwey, and Aaron Caycedo-Kimura.

Many thanks to my close friends and readers for being so patient with me, so loving, and so supportive—you know who you are.

I'd like to thank all of those people who appear in my poems, who have inspired my poems, either daily or on a whim, real or imaginary.

And finally, my eternal gratitude to my parents, sisters, and grandparents for their care, support, and love.

Notes

For the poems that appear in both Serbian and English:
*   By the Brka River
*   Vuk
*   "And during the war, especially during the war, we laughed"

All of these poems are original. I wrote these pairs of poems simultaneously in Serbian and in English, and as such, I find it crucial both versions of each poem appear together.